P9-CLK-007

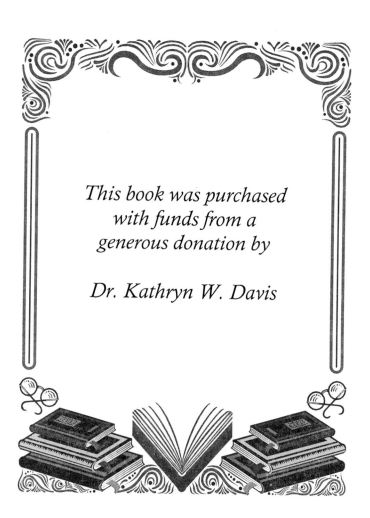

*This book was purchased
with funds from a
generous donation by*

Dr. Kathryn W. Davis

THE CHANGING CLIMATE OF

AUSTRALIA

Patricia K. Kummer

NORTH
AMERICA

EUROPE

ASIA

AFRICA

SOUTH
AMERICA

AUSTRALIA

Cavendish
Square

New York

ANTARCTICA

Published in 2014 by Cavendish Square Publishing, LLC

303 Park Avenue South, Suite 1247, New York, NY 10010

Copyright © 2014 by Cavendish Square Publishing, LLC

First Edition

No part of this publication may be reproduced, stored in a retrieval system, or transmitted in any form or by any means—electronic, me-
chanical, photocopying, recording, or otherwise—without the prior permission of the copyright owner. Request for permission should be
addressed to Permissions, Cavendish Square Publishing, 303 Park Avenue South, Suite 1247, New York, NY 10010. Tel (877) 980-4450;
fax (877) 980-4454.

Website: cavendishsq.com

This publication represents the opinions and views of the author based on his or her personal experience, knowledge, and research. The
information in this book serves as a general guide only. The author and publisher have used their best efforts in preparing this book and
disclaim liability rising directly or indirectly from the use and application of this book.

CPSIA Compliance Information: Batch #WW14CSQ

All websites were available and accurate when this book was sent to press.

Library of Congress Cataloging-in-Publication Data

Kummer, Patricia K.
The changing climate of Australia / by Patricia K. Kummer.
p. cm. — (Climates and continents)
Summary: "Provides comprehensive information on the geography, wildlife, peoples, and climate of the continent of Australia and the
changes taking place there as a result of climate change"—Provided by publisher.
Includes index.
ISBN 978-1-62712-446-1 (hardcover) ISBN 978-1-62712-447-8 (paperback) ISBN 978-1-62712-448-5 (ebook)
1. Climatic changes — Environmental aspects — Australia. I. Kummer, Patricia K. II. Title.
QC903.2.A8 K86 2014
551.6994—dc23

Editorial Director: Dean Miller
Senior Editor: Peter Mavrikis
Copy Editor: Cynthia Roby
Art Director: Jeffrey Talbot
Designer: Amy Greenan
Photo Researcher: Alison Morretta
Production Manager: Jennifer Ryder-Talbot
Production Editor: Andrew Coddington

The photographs in this book are used by permission and through the courtesy of: Cover photo by © Bill Bachman/Alamy, Davor Puk-
ljak/Shutterstock.com; Davor Pukljak/Shutterstock.com, 4; Mapping Specialists, 6; Claire Takacs/Garden Picture Library/Getty Images,
8; Mark Newman/Photo Researchers/Getty Images, 8; © Ingetje Tadros/Photonica World/Getty Images, 9; Auscape / UIG/Universal Images Group/Getty Images, 10; Mapping Specialists, 13; Richard l'Anson/Lonely Planet Images/Getty Images, 15; Robert Harding Picture
Library/SuperStock, 17; Feargus Cooney/Lonely Planet Images/Getty Images, 18; Holger Leue/Lonely Planet Images/Getty Images, 19;
Phil Walter/Staff/Getty Images News/Getty Images, 21; AP Photo/Rob Griffith, 23; Rodger Klein/WaterFrame/Getty Images, 24; Minden
Pictures/SuperStock, 27; Auscape / UIG /Universal Images Group/Getty Images, 29; Auscape/ UIG/Universal Images Group/Getty Images,
31; Reinhard Dirscherl/WaterFrame/Getty Images, 33; Andrew Watson/Photolibrary/Getty Images, 36; Ira Block/National Geographic/
Getty Images, 37; Mint Images - Frans Lanting/Mint Images/Getty Images, 37; Glenn Beanland/Lonely Planet Images/Getty Images, 38;
Manfred Gottschalk/Lonely Planet Images/Getty Images, 41.

Printed in the United States of America

CONTENTS

ONE
THE SMALLEST CONTINENT

Looking at a globe or at a world map, it is quite easy to identify the seven **continents**. They are Earth's largest areas of land. Australia is the smallest continent. It covers only about 5 percent of Earth's land. The other six continents in order of size are Asia, Africa, North America, South America, Antarctica, and Europe.

Getting To Know Australia

Australia's nickname is "The Land Down Under." The nickname is based on Australia's location—completely south of the Equator. It is the only permanently inhabited continent located there. Antarctica is the other continent that is completely south of the Equator. No permanent residents live on that icy continent, though.

(Opposite) Australia is the smallest of the seven continents. This image taken from a satellite in space shows Australia's forests (green), grasslands (orange), and deserts (tan).

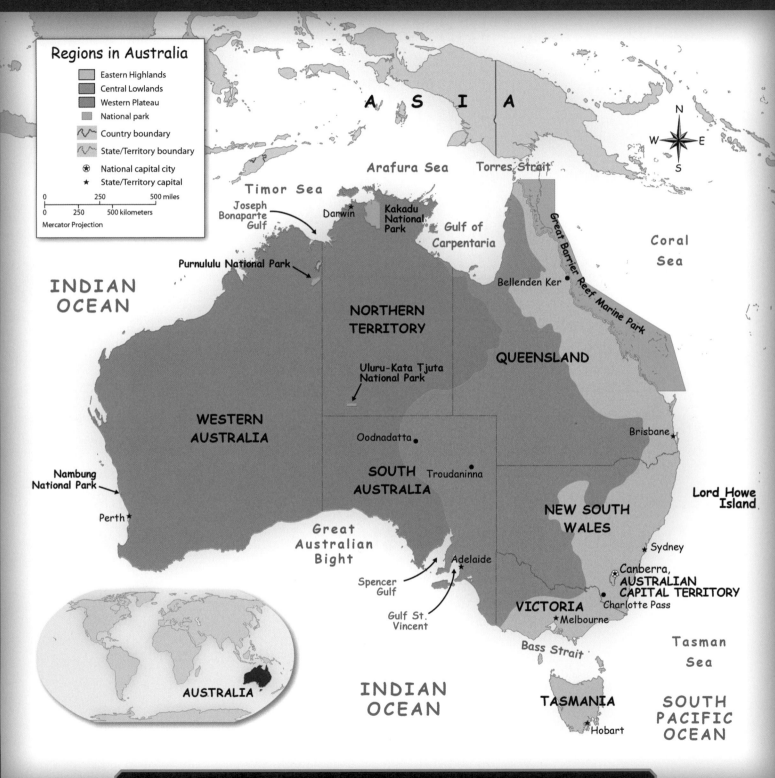

Regions in Australia

- Eastern Highlands
- Central Lowlands
- Western Plateau
- National park
- ⌇ Country boundary
- ⌇ State/Territory boundary
- ✪ National capital city
- ★ State/Territory capital

0   250   500 miles
0   250   500 kilometers
Mercator Projection

A S I A

Arafura Sea   Torres Strait

Timor Sea

Joseph Bonaparte Gulf   Darwin   Kakadu National Park   Gulf of Carpentaria   Coral Sea

Purnululu National Park

INDIAN OCEAN

Bellenden Ker

Great Barrier Reef Marine Park

NORTHERN TERRITORY

QUEENSLAND

Uluru-Kata Tjuta National Park

WESTERN AUSTRALIA

Oodnadatta

Brisbane

Nambung National Park

SOUTH AUSTRALIA   Troudaninna

NEW SOUTH WALES

Lord Howe Island

Perth ★

Great Australian Bight

Adelaide

Sydney

Spencer Gulf

Canberra, AUSTRALIAN CAPITAL TERRITORY

Gulf St. Vincent

VICTORIA   Charlotte Pass

★ Melbourne

INDIAN OCEAN

Bass Strait

Tasman Sea

AUSTRALIA

TASMANIA

SOUTH PACIFIC OCEAN

Hobart

POLITICAL MAP OF AUSTRALIA

Where in the World Is Australia?

MAPPING SKILLS

Use the political map on page 6 to answer the following questions about the continent of Australia:

1. Which continent is Australia's closest neighbor?

2. Which region covers the largest amount of Australia's land? Name the states and territories in that region.

3. Which states and territories make up the Central Lowlands?

4. What major park is on Australia's eastern coast? What bodies of water touch this park?

5. Which region is Tasmania part of?

ANSWERS:
1. Asia
2. Western Plateau; Western Australia, Northern Territory, South Australia, Queensland
3. Northern Territory, South Australia, Queensland, New South Wales, Victoria
4. Great Barrier Reef Marine Park; Torres Strait, Coral Sea
5. Eastern Highlands

The wild rose shrub is native to Western Australia.

Australia is also called an "island continent" because it is completely surrounded by water. The Timor Sea and the Arafura Sea touch Australia's northern shores. The South Pacific Ocean's Coral Sea and Tasman Sea are to the east. The Indian Ocean shapes Australia's southern and western coasts. Those seas and oceans separate Australia from other continents.

Australia has three main landform regions—the Eastern Highlands, the Central Lowlands, and the Western Plateau. The Eastern Highlands have Australia's highest land, mildest climate, and largest population. The continent's lowest land and longest rivers are found in the Central Lowlands. The Western Plateau has Australia's flattest land, largest deserts, and smallest number of people.

Australia's location and landforms make Australia's climate the driest of the permanently inhabited continents. The continent's landforms and climate, in

The red kangaroo is the largest mammal in Australia.

Australia's Aboriginals have used art as a form of expression for thousands of years.

turn, provide **habitats** for unusual plants and animals. Many of them, such as the Tasmanian devil, are only found in Australia.

Australia is also unique because it is the only continent that is also a country. The country of Australia is the world's sixth largest nation. It is made up of six states—Queensland, New South Wales, South Australia, Tasmania, Victoria, and Western Australia—and two territories—the Australian Capital Territory (A.C.T.) and the Northern Territory. Several islands are also part of Australia. Tasmania is the largest of the islands.

Among the continents, Australia's population ranks sixth in size. Only Antarctica has fewer people. The people of Australia belong to many **ethnic groups**. Aboriginals and Torres Straits Islanders are Australia's indigenous (native) people. Most Australians, however, trace their families back to Europe, Asia, New Zealand, and the Americas.

Uluru — A Huge Red Rock

In the middle of Australia, Uluru, also known as Ayers Rock, rises 1,142 feet (348 m) above the desert. It is almost 6 miles (9.6 km) around at its base. In addition to its size above the desert floor, Uluru is thought to extend more than 3 miles (4.8 km) underground. This red sandstone **monolith** is the world's largest single rock. Uluru's red color comes from iron that is in the sandstone. As the light changes during the day, Uluru can look red, orange, pink, purple, or blue.

Uluru is what remains of an ancient mountain range. Through millions of years, wind and water wore down the mountains. About 325 million years ago, tectonic movement tilted Uluru upward into its current position.

Every year, thousands of visitors travel to see Uluru. Some of them walk completely around the huge rock. During the three-to-four-hour walk, they can look into shallow caves that have formed. The caves' walls have paintings made by ancient Aboriginal people.

The Continents and Change

For hundreds of millions of years, Australia and the other continents have undergone slow, continuous change. In fact about 250 million years ago, there was only one continent—Pangaea. Gradually, Pangaea broke apart. About 50 million years ago, Australia separated from Antarctica. It began moving north until it reached its current location.

Movement of Earth's **tectonic plates** causes the continents' locations and landforms to change. Each continent sits on a tectonic plate. Australia is in the middle of the Australian Plate. Tectonic movement pushed up Australia's mountains and formed volcanoes. Australia's volcanoes are now **extinct**. Tectonic movement continues to push Australia north. Every year, this continent moves about 3 inches (8 cm) closer to Asia.

Another kind of change that concerns Australia and the other continents is **climate change**. The main cause of climate change is the release of large amounts of carbon dioxide (CO_2) into the air. Natural events such as volcanic eruptions add to the air's CO_2. Human activities such as burning coal, oil, natural gas, and gasoline also emit CO_2. In addition, altering the natural environment can release more CO_2. For example, Australian ranchers have allowed cattle and sheep to overgraze grasslands, which absorb CO_2. Warmer temperatures and varying rainfall often result from those activities. Now, some of Australia's leaders are working to improve the environment. Their actions will still bring more changes to Australia.

TWO

A LOW, FLAT, AND DRY LAND

Australia is the lowest, flattest, and almost driest of the seven continents. Its average elevation is only 1,083 feet (330 m) above sea level. Australia's land also has the smallest difference between its highest and lowest points. Except for Antarctica, Australia receives the least annual precipitation of the continents.

The low, flat features of Australia developed because the continent is located in the middle of the Australian Plate. This location has prevented mountain building from continuing. The continent's dry climate resulted from the lack of high mountains and from having only a few deep bays and gulfs.

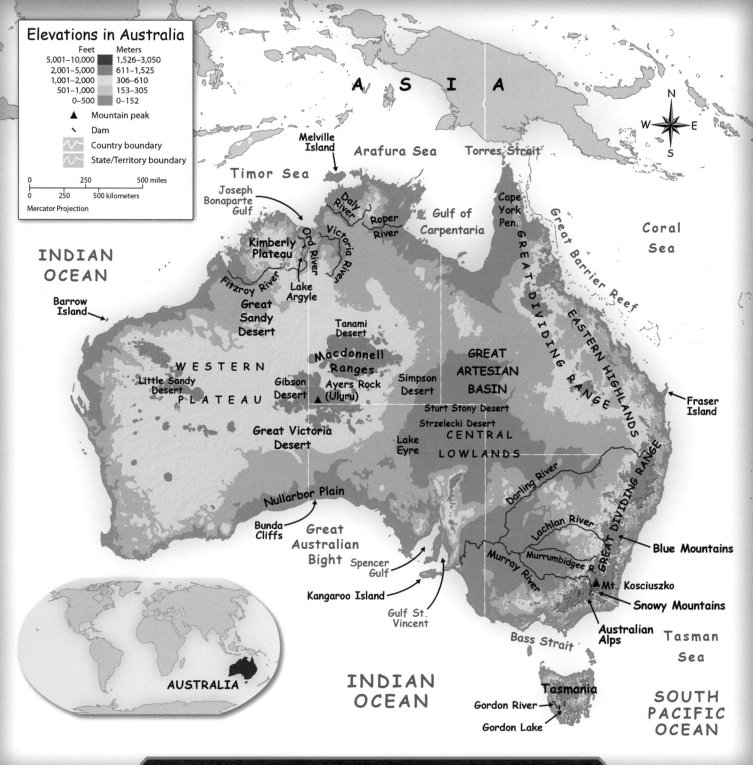

Elevations in Australia

Feet	Meters
5,001–10,000	1,526–3,050
2,001–5,000	611–1,525
1,001–2,000	306–610
501–1,000	153–305
0–500	0–152

▲ Mountain peak
\ Dam
Country boundary
State/Territory boundary

0   250   500 miles
0   250   500 kilometers

Mercator Projection

ASIA

Arafura Sea
Torres Strait
Timor Sea
Melville Island
Joseph Bonaparte Gulf
Daly River
Roper River
Gulf of Carpentaria
Cape York Pen.
Coral Sea
Great Barrier Reef

INDIAN OCEAN

Kimberly Plateau
Ord River
Victoria River
Fitzroy River
Lake Argyle
Great Sandy Desert
Barrow Island
Tanami Desert

WESTERN

Little Sandy Desert
Macdonnell Ranges
Gibson Desert
Ayers Rock (Uluru)
Simpson Desert

GREAT ARTESIAN BASIN

PLATEAU
Great Victoria Desert
Sturt Stony Desert
Strzelecki Desert
Lake Eyre

CENTRAL LOWLANDS

GREAT DIVIDING RANGE
EASTERN HIGHLANDS

Fraser Island

Nullarbor Plain
Bunda Cliffs
Great Australian Bight
Spencer Gulf
Kangaroo Island
Gulf St. Vincent
Darling River
Lachlan River
Murray River
Murrumbidgee R.
Blue Mountains
Mt. Kosciuszko
Snowy Mountains
Australian Alps

GREAT DIVIDING RANGE

Bass Strait

Tasman Sea

INDIAN OCEAN

Tasmania
Gordon River
Gordon Lake

SOUTH PACIFIC OCEAN

AUSTRALIA

PHYSICAL MAP OF AUSTRALIA

Getting the Lay of the Land

MAPPING SKILLS

Study the physical map of Australia on page 13 to answer the following questions:

1. In the winter, what kind of precipitation would you expect to find in the Australian Alps and the Snowy Mountains? Why?

2. Why do you think there are no major rivers on the Western Plateau?

3. What landform prevents Australia's major rivers from flowing into the Tasman Sea?

4. Which deserts are in the Central Lowlands?

ANSWERS: 1. Snow; The European Alps are known for snow, and Snowy Mountains likely got their name from snow on them. 2. Deserts cover much of that area. 3. Great Dividing Range, or Eastern Highlands 4. Simpson, Sturt Stony, Strzelecki

Hanging Rock, a landmark in Blue Mountains National Park, is part of the Eastern Highlands in New South Wales, Australia.

The Eastern Highlands

The Eastern Highlands covers only 15 percent of Australia. This region has the continent's highest mountains, largest forests, best farmland, and largest cities. The Eastern Highlands is also called the Great Dividing Range. This range determines the direction in which the region's rivers flow. Short, fast-flowing rivers rush down the eastern slopes into the Coral or Tasman seas. Long, slow-moving rivers flow down the western slopes and cross the Central Lowlands.

The Great Dividing Range is actually made up of several separate ranges. The Australian Alps is the largest range and includes Australia's tallest peak. Mount Kosciuszko rises 7,310 feet (2,228 m) above sea level in the Alps' Snowy Mountains. Between the ranges of the eastern mountains lie plateaus and low hills.

Long ago, lava and ash from volcanic eruptions created rich soil on the plateaus and hills. Now, rain falls year-round on those lands. Good soil and rainfall enable forests, grasses, and crops to grow well in this region. In addition, the region's milder climate has encouraged the cities of Sydney, Brisbane, and Melbourne to flourish.

15

The Central Lowlands

About 25 percent of Australia is covered by the Central Lowlands. This region has Australia's lowest land. Much of the Central Lowlands is also dry land. Deserts lie in the west-central part of the lowlands. Most of the region's rain falls at its northern tip and along the western slopes of the Eastern Highlands. Australia's longest rivers flow down those slopes and then cross the Central Lowlands. Most of the rivers are dry except during the summer rains. Large, mainly dry, salt lakes are also found in the lowlands.

Most of this region's water lies underground in the Great Artesian Basin. Throughout the lowlands, this water is piped aboveground. Unfortunately, the water has a high level of salt. People cannot drink this water, and it cannot be used for irrigating crops. Cattle can drink the water, though. It is also used by the region's mining industry.

The Western Plateau

The Western Plateau covers about 60 percent of Australia. This region is higher than the Central Lowlands. It also has some of the continent's flattest and driest land. Almost 50 percent of the Western Plateau is desert. Australia's largest deserts cover most of the central part of the plateau. Few people live in that area. Almost no farming or grazing takes place there either.

The northern, southwestern, and southeastern tips of the Western Plateau receive the greatest rainfall. Harvests of wheat, corn, fruits, and vegetables come from this well-watered soil. It also produces grasses for dairy cows and sheep to graze on. This region has three large cities— Adelaide, Perth, and Darwin. They are also found at the extreme tips of the Western Plateau.

The Murray River flows through grassland in Victoria.

Rivers, Lakes, and Coastlines

Australia has only a few long rivers. Little rainfall causes many of them to run dry during much of the year. The Western Plateau's few rivers are at the plateau's southern tip and farther north on the Kimberley Plateau.

The continent's three longest rivers each start in the Eastern Highlands. They all flow west across the Central Lowlands. The Darling is Australia's longest river at 1,702 miles (2,739 km). Low rainfall prevents it from flowing in the winter, though. When the summer rains fall, the Darling then flows into the Murray River. The Murray is Australia's longest permanently flowing river. From the Snowy Mountains, the Murray flows 1,609 miles (2,589 km) into the Indian Ocean near Adelaide, South Australia. The continent's third-longest river, the Murrumbidgee, flows from the Snowy Mountains into the Murray River. Water from the Murray and Murrumbidgee rivers is used to irrigate the

The Nullarbor Plain

On the Western Plateau, the Nullarbor Plain stretches along Australia's southern coast. This plain's name means "no trees"—and there are no trees on it. That is why Australians affectionately call it the "Nullar-boring." The Nullarbor is Earth's largest piece of limestone. It was an ancient seabed that was thrust upward by tectonic movement. During millions of years, wind and rain have worn down the limestone to a flat plain. This open, flat land allowed Australia to build the world's

longest straight line of railroad. It runs for almost 300 miles (483 km) without a curve.

Every year, many Australians take the train or drive the Eyre Highway across the Nullarbor. Then they check that accomplishment off their to-do list. Along the way, many people stop at the Bunda Cliffs. From these 295-foot- (90-m-) high limestone cliffs, they sometimes sight whales in the Great Australian Bight. Under the cliffs, the ocean has eaten away the limestone. This erosion has created the world's longest cave system. It extends miles (km) inland under the Nullarbor Plain. Entrance to the caves is through holes that have formed on top of the plain.

southern Central Lowlands. Irrigation has increased the amount of land that can support crops and grazing.

Australia's largest lakes are salt lakes. They are usually dry and completely fill only once or twice every 100 years. Lake Eyre, the largest of those lakes, is also Australia's lowest point—52 feet (16 m) below sea level. The continent's major freshwater lakes are reservoirs. They were created by dams built on rivers. Lake Argyle in far northwestern Australia and Lake Gordon in Tasmania are the largest of those lakes.

Australia's coastline of 37,118 miles (59,736 km) includes beaches, cliffs, and forestlands. Wide, sandy beaches stretch along the eastern coast. Offshore from northern Queensland lies the Great Barrier Reef. Rough waves pound the beaches of the western coast. High cliffs rise over the southern coast. Palm trees and mangrove forests grow along the northern coast.

The Bunda Cliffs rise up over the Great Australian Bight in Nullarbor National Park along Australia's southern coast.

WARMING TEMPERATURES, VARYING RAINFALL

Located south of the Equator, Australia is completely in the Southern Hemisphere. Part of Africa and South America and all of Antarctica are also in that **hemisphere**. North America and Europe and most of Asia are in the Northern Hemisphere. The seasons occur differently on the continents in those two hemispheres. For example, when Australians are enjoying summer, it is winter in North America. Climate zones also are arranged differently. In Australia, temperatures are warmer in the north and become cooler in the south. In the Northern Hemisphere, temperatures are cooler in the north and become warmer in the south.

Of the six permanently inhabited continents, Australia has the fewest climate zones. The Tropic of Capricorn runs through northern Australia. That gives the northern part of the continent a hot, wet tropical climate. Australia's largest annual rainfall—316.3 inches (803 cm)—occurs in

Bellenden Ker, Queensland. The rest of Australia's eastern coast and much of the southern coast have warm to hot temperatures. In the winter, however, low temperatures and snow hit Australia's Snowy Mountains. Charlotte Pass, New South Wales, recorded the continent's lowest temperature of -9.4°F (-22°C) in 1994.

In contrast, a dry, hot desert climate exists throughout most of the middle of the continent. That's where Australia's highest temperatures and lowest precipitation occur. Oodnadatta holds the continent's record high of 123°F (50°C), reached in 1960. Troudaninna receives the least rain each year—4.05 inches (10 cm). Both of those places are in South Australia.

A scientist takes a cutting from a rainforest tree to study the effects of climate change.

Climate Change in Australia

Major differences in temperatures and precipitation over several years are known as climate change. Human activities are responsible for most of Australia's climate change. During the 1800s, people who had **emigrated** from Europe began making major changes to the land. They cut down forests along the eastern coast and planted crops instead. They also brought sheep and cattle to Australia. Those flocks and herds overgrazed Australia's grasslands. Trees and grasses absorb CO_2. With fewer forests and grasslands, the amount of CO_2 in the air increased. That in turn has caused temperatures to increase and rainfall to decrease.

Australians have also built large cities along the coasts. These urban areas create heat islands. Heat builds up in urban areas because the land is covered by buildings, streets, and roads. On hot, sunny days, Australia's cities can be as much as 9°F (5°C) warmer than nearby rural areas.

In addition, Australia's homes, apartments, factories, and office buildings must be cooled and heated. Most of Australia's electricity is generated from coal-burning power plants. Cars, buses, trains, and trucks use gasoline or diesel fuel. All of those fuels give off CO_2, which adds to climate change.

Results of Climate Change

During the past 100 years, Australia has experienced climate change. Overall in Australia, temperatures have become warmer by 1.6°F (0.9°C). That is more than the world's average increase of 1.3°F (0.74°C). Temperatures in the eastern and central parts of Australia have increased the most. Warmer temperatures already are speeding up the melting of snow in the Australian Alps. Southern Australia is experiencing more frequent and longer heat waves.

The pattern of precipitation in Australia has changed, too. The northwestern and northeastern tips of Australia are receiving heavier rainfalls. This has caused severe flooding in some cities. In contrast, less

A baby koala has its weight checked at Wildlife Sydney Zoo.

rain now falls on southwestern and southeastern Australia. Victoria's annual rainfall has decreased by 4.3 inches (11 cm). Drier conditions in the southeast have led to longer **droughts** and more wildfires.

Another effect of climate change is warming of ocean waters. As the oceans become warmer, their water expands. This in turn causes sea levels to rise. Higher sea levels have already occurred along Australia's western and southern coasts.

How Scientists Measure Climate Change

Australian scientists use many methods to measure climate change. Some of them study the climate in Australia's past. For example, scientists in the Australian Alps are examining 15,000-year-old plant material from deep peat bogs. This ancient matter helps explain climate change through many years. Other scientists observe and record changes in animal behavior. In the mountains of Australia's rainforest, many birds, frogs, and tree possums have moved to higher elevations. Those animals are seeking cooler and wetter habitats. Their former homes have become warmer and drier.

The Great Barrier Reef

The Great Barrier Reef is located in the Coral Sea. It stretches 1,428 miles (2,300 km) next to Australia's northeastern coast. Made up of about 3,000 reefs, this is the world's largest coral reef system.

About 18 million years ago, coral polyps began building the reef. Coral polyps are tiny, soft animals. They attach themselves to hard surfaces on the ocean floor to begin building a reef. When they die, their hardened skeletons become part of the reef. Then, more polyps attach themselves to the

reef. More than 400 kinds of coral live on the Great Barrier Reef. About 1,500 kinds of fish and many other sea animals also make their homes on it.

Coral polyps eat a plant called zooxanthellae. This plant needs sunlight in which to grow. That is why coral reefs grow near the surface in warm seawater. But zooxanthellae die when the water gets too warm. In recent years, the water temperature around the Great Barrier Reef has increased about 0.7°F (0.4°C). This has led to coral bleaching in which large parts of the reef turn white and die. The coral dies because its food—zooxanthellae—has died. Coral bleaching has been occurring more often. If this continues, some scientists believe that the Great Barrier Reef could become extinct by 2030.

Natural Disasters

Australia frequently experiences weather-related natural disasters. Between November and April, **cyclones** often hit Australia's northern coast. These windstorms develop over the Indian Ocean's warm water. Warm, wet air rises from the ocean and starts spinning. When cyclones make landfall, their winds cause much damage. The winds can reach 200 miles (322 km) per hour. Heavy rains from the storms cause severe floods. With ocean waters becoming warmer, cyclones are occurring more frequently and with fiercer winds. In 2011, Cyclone Yasi destroyed trees and banana and sugarcane crops in Queensland.

Another wind, called a **monsoon**, blows down from Asia. Monsoons bring heavy rains that cause flooding. From November 2010 through January 2011, monsoon rains fell on Queensland, New South Wales, Victoria, and South Australia. Rivers overflowed and streets filled with water. Several people died from the flooding. Many others lost their homes.

Wildfires are another kind of natural disaster. They frequently occur in dry areas of Victoria and South Australia. High temperatures, strong winds, and dry brush and grass cause wildfires to break out. In February 2009, a wildfire raced across Victoria. In the end, 173 people were killed, 500 people were injured, more than 2,000 homes were destroyed, and millions of wildlife died. If climate change continues, Australia can expect more of these natural disasters.

FOUR

A CHANGING NATURAL ENVIRONMENT

Because Australia is an island continent, its plants and animals developed differently from those on the other continents. Australia's **marsupials** are its best-known animals. They include the bilby, kangaroo, koala, Tasmanian devil, wallaby, and wombat.

Since people first came to Australia, they have made changes to the natural environment. In turn, those changes have damaged the habitats of many of Australia's plants and animals. Today, some of the remaining plant and animal species are endangered.

Fewer Forests

Tropical rainforests line Australia's northern and northeastern coasts. More than 80 inches (203 cm) of rain falls on them each year. Mangrove trees with their long, aboveground roots grow near the shores. Fish,

The Southern cassowary, a relative of the ostrich and the emu, lives in Australia's rainforests.

shrimp, frogs, and other sea animals live among the roots. Deeper in the rainforest, kauri, laurel, maple, palm, and red cedar trees flourish. Vines, such as strangler figs and rattan palm, wrap themselves around the trees. The main animals of the rainforest are birds such as the flightless cassowary and golden bowerbird. Other animals include the tree kangaroo and mahogany glider.

The Blue Mountains of New South Wales have large areas of eucalyptus forests. Golden wattle trees grow beneath the eucalyptus. Banksias plants flood the forest floor with bright colors. Eucalyptus trees and banksias need fires every ten to twenty years to release their seeds. Within a few years, new trees and plants begin to grow. Recently, more frequent fires are preventing regrowth. Koalas are the main animals in the eucalyptus forests. The trees' leaves provide koalas with both food and water. Kookaburras perch on the eucalyptus trees' high branches.

Tasmania's forests have tall myrtle beech, sassafras, and several species of pine trees. Tree ferns grow beneath the taller trees. Animals such as the Tasmanian devil, Tasmanian long-tailed mouse, and ringtail possum live in the forests.

Since the 1800s, about 50 percent of Australia's forests have disappeared. The trees were cut down for their lumber. Forestland soon gave way to farmland, mines, roads, and cities. Large areas of Tasmania's forest were cut when dams were built. All of these activities caused many animals to lose their habitats. Now, the cassowary, koala, and Tasmanian devil are **endangered species**. The King Billy Pine is an endangered tree. However, **deforestation** continues in the forests in Queensland and Tasmania.

Changing Grasslands

Australia's grasslands form a backward "C" through the continent. They lie between the northern and eastern forests and the central deserts. In the northern grasslands, tussock grasses grow in clumps. Kangaroo grass and Mitchell's grass can grow several feet high. Shrubs and small trees appear among the grasses. Gray kangaroos and wallabies feed on these plants. In the southeastern grasslands, groups of eucalyptus and paperbark trees stand out. Cockatoos, kookaburras, parakeets, and parrots roost in the eucalyptus trees. They live off seeds found among the grasses. In southwestern Australia, scrubland supports dwarf eucalyptus trees and mulga shrubs. Blue bush and saltbush also grow there.

Kakadu National Park

Kakadu National Park is located in the far northern tip of the Northern Territory. The park has rainforest, savanna, wetlands, and rock formations. Mangrove trees line the northern edge of park. Eucalyptus trees and grasses are found throughout the park. Wetlands form when the area's rivers and creeks flood from the monsoon rains. After the rains, water plunges over high sandstone cliffs. Jim Jim Falls and Twin Falls Gorge attract many visitors. People also take boat rides on billabongs—freshwater inland lagoons. The world's only freshwater crocodiles live in them. Huge saltwater crocodiles share those waters. Barramundi also swim there. Saltwater crocodiles compete with people to catch these 200-pound (91 kg) fish.

Some of the world's richest uranium, gold, and platinum deposits lie under the park's land. The Ranger Uranium Mine operates at the eastern edge of the park. The mining company follows guidelines to protect the environment. It also set up a special fund to clean up the site when mining stops.

Several animals make homes throughout the grasslands. Termites build mounds several feet high. Echidnas, also called spiny anteaters, peck at the mounds. These anteaters belong to one of only two species of mammals that lay eggs and hatch their young. Flightless emus, the world's second-largest birds, can be seen quickly running across the grasslands. Dingoes prey on kangaroos and other grassland animals.

Much of the grasslands are now used for farming or grazing. Cattle ranches cover the northern grasslands. Sheep graze on grasses and shrubs in the south. Other parts of the southern grasslands have become huge wheat fields. Overgrazing and turning grassland into farmland has led to **desertification**. This occurs when overused soil receives little rainfall. The topsoil dries up and blows away. The soil that remains is too weak to support crops or grass.

Wetter Deserts

Deserts receive less than 10 inches (25 cm) of rain each year. This lack of water prevents trees from growing there. But the boab is a tree that grows in the northwestern desert. During the spring rains, the boab stores water in its large trunk until the next rainfall. Moisture also causes the desert to burst into color for short periods. The scarlet flowers of the Sturt's Desert pea plant push between the rocks on the Sturt Stony Desert. In other parts of the western desert, red and green kangaroo paw and golden feather flowers bloom. The main plants in Australia's vast deserts, however, are short, tufted grasses. The roots of spinifex and cane grass hold the desert sands together.

Some of the world's most poisonous snakes, such as the desert death adder, king brown snake, and taipan, slither through Australia's deserts. Lizards, such as the monitor, perenties, and frill-necked, scamper about.

Rat-kangaroos, red kangaroos, wombats, and bilbies are some of the deserts largest animals.

The greater bilby is a threatened species. The lesser bilby became extinct in the 1950s.

Bilbies and wombats dig burrows in which they live during the heat of the day. Rodents, such as jerba-rats and hare-wallabies, make homes there, too. Dingoes live in the desert, too. They prey on the other desert animals.

In recent years, rainfall on parts of the northwestern desert has increased 4 to 12 inches (10–30 cm) each year. This has allowed farmers to irrigate that land and to plant crops on it. Grasses now grow there, too. Ranchers have cattle graze on the grasses. As these activities increase, some desert plants and animals will lose their habitats.

Menacing Invasive Species

In the 1800s, Europeans brought camels, pet cats, foxes, and rabbits to Australia. At that time, camels provided transportation across Australia's huge deserts. Today groups of wild camels trample grasslands. Rabbits and foxes provided game for hunting. The rabbits have since destroyed large areas of trees and shrubs by gnawing bark on low branches. Cats and foxes now prey on bilbies and other small mammals. In the 1930s, cane toads were brought to Australia to kill beetles that were ruining the sugarcane crops. Now the toads also prey on native Australian bees and smaller toads. In recent years, Australia's government has passed laws that prevent people from bringing animals to the continent.

Lakes, Rivers, and Coastal Waters

Australia's lakes, rivers, and coastal waters provide habitats for thousands of birds, fish, and other water animals. When Australia's usually dry lakes receive water, pelicans, magpie geese, and ducks flock to their shores. In eastern Australia, duck-billed platypuses live in rivers and streams. They are the other species of mammals that lay eggs and hatch their young.

Saltwater crocodiles, sharks, and whales ply the coastal waters. White-bellied sea eagles, goshawks, and ospreys soar overhead. They build nests high on coastal cliffs. Petrels and albatrosses feast on squid. Herons and egrets pick up

Saltwater crocodiles are the largest crocodiles on Earth. They can grow to be more than 20 feet (6 m) long and can weigh up to 2,220 pounds (1,000 kg).

clams, crabs, fish, and frogs among mangrove roots. Boobies pluck flying fish from the air.

Through the years, many of Australia's waters have become polluted. Fertilizers from farms have washed into rivers. The same thing has happened with waste produced by cattle and sheep, by mining operations, and by cities. When these polluted river waters flow into the oceans and seas, the coastal land and water becomes polluted. In the Coral Sea, waste discharges from ships have damaged parts of the Great Barrier Reef. This pollution makes it hard for fish and other animals to survive. It also threatens the main catches of Australia's fishing industry—black marlin, yellowfin tuna, lobsters, and shrimp.

FIVE

PEOPLE AND CHANGE

Australia is a continent of immigrants. About 50,000 years ago, Australia's first people arrived. They are called Aboriginals. About 10,000 years ago, people from the Torres Straits Islands began moving onto the continent. Today, about 2 percent of Australians can trace their ancestors back to those first groups of people.

In 1788, Europeans—mainly British and Irish—started settling in Australia. From the late 1800s to the present day, Australia's population groups have expanded. They now include people whose families once lived throughout Europe, Asia, New Zealand, and the Americas.

Australia's warm climate, natural resources, and strong economy have made the continent a good place for people to live. Currently of the continents, Australia has the world's sixth-largest population. About 23 million people live there. By 2025, Australia's population is expected to be about 25 million. By 2050, that number could reach about 29 million.

Changes in Population Growth

Australia's population is increasing by 1.2 percent each year. Much of the growth is from immigration. Australia's strong economy continues to attract immigrants. A large number of immigrants now come from China, India, and Southeast Asia. They are sure that they will find well-paying jobs. They also want their children to receive high-quality educations that Australia's schools and universities offer. Australia's high level of health care is another attraction.

The growth rate of Australia's nonimmigrant population is low, however. People are having fewer children. Most Australians graduate from high school and go to college or to a technical school. Then, they establish their careers before getting married and having children.

Australia also has an aging population. People are living longer. The average life expectancy for Australians is 81 years. This is due mainly to improved health care. However, the average life span of Aboriginals is only 65 years. Many Aboriginals still live in poverty and do not have access to health care.

Where Australia's People Live

About 90 percent of Australia's people live in urban areas—large cities and their suburbs. That makes Australia the most-urbanized continent. Highly populated cities and large towns developed on the continent's

Like this couple in Perth, Western Australia, about 80 percent of all Australians can trace their families' roots to Europe.

coasts. About 50 percent of all Australians live in the eastern cities of Sydney, Brisbane, and Melbourne. Recently, smaller towns have been built west of these large urban areas. People who live in those towns commute to work in the cities.

The other 10 percent of Australians live on farms and ranches or in small towns in the countryside. Rural areas in Australia are called "the bush." Rural Australians work as farmers, ranchers, or miners. They produce food for Australia's people and raw materials for its industries. In the tropics of Australia, farmers grow large crops of bananas, pineapples, and sugarcane. In drier parts of Australia, they harvest large barley, oat, and wheat crops. On sheep ranches, workers shear tons (t) of wool each year. Australia's miners produce some of the world's largest amounts of aluminum, coal, diamonds, opals, and uranium.

A Once Endangered People — Australia's Aboriginals

When the British came to Australia, up to 1 million Aboriginals lived throughout the continent. They made up about 500 different groups, each with its own land area and language. Most Aboriginals lived along the northern and eastern coasts. The British and other Europeans took over all the land. Gradually, the Aboriginals were pushed into the hot, dry **outback**. Some historians believe that by 1900, the Aboriginal population had dropped to about 60,000. Wars, disease, and loss of their native foods accounted for the decrease. The British also took Aboriginal children away from their parents. The children were sent to special schools. There they received British names and were forced to speak English. Many forgot their native languages.

Since the 1970s, the Australian government has granted land rights back to Aboriginal groups. Their living conditions, educations, and health care have improved somewhat. Today, about 460,000 Aboriginals live in Australia. Most of them live in cities in Queensland and New South Wales. About 100 Aboriginal languages still exist. Only about twenty of them are spoken, though.

Sydney — Australia's Largest City

Sydney is Australia's oldest and largest city. Located on a huge harbor, Sydney is also the capital New South Wales. Moderate temperatures and rainfall have attracted people to the area for thousands of years. In 1788, Britain established Sydney as a place for British prisoners. Today, the people of Sydney are called "Sydneysiders."

In 2013, about 4.7 million people lived in Sydney. That is about 20 percent of all Australians. Many Sydneysiders work in the electronics, food processing, garment and textile, papermaking, and shipbuilding industries. Other Sydneysiders work in advertising, banking, insurance, tourism, and trade. Today, ships leave Sydney's harbor and carry Australian exports of coal, fruit, meat from cattle and sheep, timber, wheat, and wool to all parts of the world.

Millions of people visit Sydney every year. One of the first things they see is the huge Sydney Harbor Bridge. Every day, hundreds of people take special walking tours up through the arch of the bridge. Another famous sight is the Sydney Opera House. Its white roofs look like a ship's sails. This building has become a symbol for the entire country. Both visitors and Sydneysiders enjoy nearby beaches. Waves from the Tasman Sea are perfect for surfing.

SIX

LOOKING FOR SOLUTIONS TO PRESENT-DAY PROBLEMS

Australia has a growing population with little livable land for people to expand onto. The continent's people also struggle between protecting the natural environment and developing natural resources.

Australia's Major Problems

One of Australia's major problems is its population. The growing population puts more pressure on its coastal cities. However, people cannot just move to the bush or to the outback. High temperatures, dry land, and little water prevent those areas from supporting more people. In addition, Australia's population is getting older. By 2050, the percentage of people over 65 years of age will be greater than the percentage of people under 15 years of age. That means that fewer young people will be available to support the elderly. As people age, they put more strain on the health care and pension systems.

39

Deforestation is another problem. Throughout eastern Australia, large amounts of forest continue to be cut. In Queensland, they are removed so miners can reach natural gas found in seams of coal. In Tasmania, tin, lead, and zinc mines replace the trees.

Another problem that Australia, along with the rest of the world, must face is climate change. By 2030, scientists predict temperatures throughout Australia to rise by 1.8°F (1°C). Rainfall is predicted to decrease by about 5 percent. Drought throughout the continent is expected to increase by about 30 percent. More severe droughts are expected in eastern Australia. They are predicted to occur more frequently in the southeast. If these predictions prove true, Australia can expect more wildfires. Future wildfires will be stronger, faster, and harder to put out. In addition, the continued rise of sea levels will threaten Australia's coastal cities. Large numbers of people will then have to move farther inland. This will hurt the environments of the bush and outback.

Toward a Better Tomorrow

Australia does have several things in its favor. The continent has many well-educated people. They provide leadership for Australia's government and businesses. They also provide workers for Australia's industries.

The continent also has some of the world's richest deposits of mineral resources. The world's largest bauxite (aluminum) mine is on the Cape York Peninsula. The Kimberley Plateau has the world's largest

Pinnacles and Bungle Bungles

Western Australia has two national parks with extreme landforms. Nambung National Park is on the southwestern coast north of Perth. This park is famous for limestone pillars, called Pinnacles. They rise up from the sand dunes and stand as high as 15 feet (4.5 m) tall. The Pinnacles are roots of ancient coastal plants that bonded with the sand through thousands of years. Now they are fossils. Visitors may walk among the Pinnacles but should not touch them.

Purnululu National Park is in the northwest on the Kimberley Plateau. Its black and orange tiger-striped sandstone domes look like beehives. They are called the Bungle Bungles. During millions of years, striping occurred through layering of rock and black lichens. Climbing the Bungle Bungles is forbidden.

diamond mine. Huge iron ore and uranium mines lie in South Australia. Queensland has large deposits of coal. Coal and iron ore contribute to Australia's steel industry. Although the continent has a small percentage of good cropland, large amounts of the world's barley, oats, sugarcane, and wheat are grown on Australia's farms.

Australia's government is acting to reduce the amount of coal used to produce electricity. Attempts are being made to use cleaner, more natural sources of energy, such as wind and solar power. Solar power comes from the sun. Wind farms with wind turbines—modern-day windmills—stand throughout Australia in places with strong, steady winds. South Australia produces the most wind power. In 2012, the continent's first solar power plant opened in Western Australia.

To protect large areas of the natural environment, Australia's government has established more than 500 national parks. They are found along the coasts, in rainforests, and in deserts. Some of the parks are co-managed by the government and local Aboriginals.

GLOSSARY

climate change — an increase or decrease in temperature or rainfall over a long period of time

continent — a large land mass

cyclone — a storm with damaging winds and heavy rain that hits land bordering the Indian Ocean

deforestation — cutting down of entire forests

desertification — weakening of soil from deforestation, drought, overuse of land, or climate change

drought — a long period of time with little or no rainfall, making it hard to grow crops

emigrate — to leave one land to live in another land

endangered species — a plant or animal that is in danger of becoming extinct

ethnic group — people who share the same national origins, language, and culture

extinct — no longer active, such as a volcano; no longer existing, such as a species of plant or animal

habitat

the natural place in which a plant or animal lives

hemisphere

one half of Earth, such as the Eastern, Northern, Southern, or Western hemisphere

marsupial

a mammal whose females carry their young in a pouch

monolith

a single large rock

monsoon

a strong wind that brings heavy rain

outback

the area of deserts and grasslands in the central part of Australia where few people live

tectonic plates

the hard sheets of moving rock that make up Earth's crust

FIND OUT MORE

BOOKS

Debnam, Mio and Tania Willis. *KidsGo! Sydney: Tell Your Parents Where to Go*. KidsGo! Guide. Hong Kong: Haven Books, 2012.

Kummer, Patricia K. *The Great Barrier Reef*. Nature's Wonders. Tarrytown, New York: Marshall Cavendish Benchmark, 2009.

Lewin, Ted and Betsy Lewin. *Top to Bottom Down Under*. New York: HarperCollins Publishers, 2005.

Wojahn, Rebecca Hogue. *An Australia Outback Food Chain: A Who-Eats-What Adventure.* Follow That Food Chain. Minneapolis: Lerner Publications, 2009.

Woodward, John. *Climate Change*. Eyewitness Books. New York: DK Publishing, 2008.

DVDS

Australia the Beautiful. Reader's Digest: Must See Places of the World. Chicago: Questar, 2009.

Great Barrier Reef. London: BBC Worldwide Ltd., 2013.

WEBSITES

Australia – http://australia.gov.au
The official Australia website with everything you want to know about the land down under—the land, people, culture, and government.

Animals—Australian Museum – http://australianmuseum.net.au/animals
Link to fact sheets, photos, and more for information about Australia's diverse animals.

INDEX

ABOUT THE AUTHOR

Patricia K. Kummer has a B.A. in history from St. Catherine University in St. Paul, Minnesota, and an M.A. in history from Marquette University in Milwaukee, Wisconsin. She has written chapters for several world history and American history textbooks and has authored more than sixty books about countries, states, natural wonders, inventions, and other topics. Books she has written for Cavendish Square include *Working Horses* in the Horses! series and the seven books in the Climates and Continents series.